THE H
FU

THE HIPPO BOOK OF FUNNY VERSE

compiled by Beverley Mathias
illustrated by Tony Kenyon

Hippo Books
Scholastic Publications Limited
London

For Anne Atrocious
who knew most of them

Scholastic Publications Ltd.,
10 Earlham Street, London WC2H 9RX, UK.

Scholastic Inc.,
730 Broadway, New York, NY 10003, USA

Scholastic Tab Publications Ltd.,
123 Newkirk Road, Richmond Hill,
Ontario L4C 3G5, Canada

Ashton Scholastic Pty. Ltd.,
P O Box 579, Gosford, New South Wales.
Australia

Ashton Scholastic Ltd.,
165 Marua Road, Panmure, Auckland 6,
New Zealand

This collection first published by Scholastic Publications Ltd., 1987
Collection copyright © Scholastic Publications Limited, 1987
Illustrations copyright © Tony Kenyon, 1987

For copyright of individual poems, please see Acknowledgements

ISBN O 590 70677 2

All rights reserved

Typeset in Souvenir by AKM Associates (UK) Ltd,
Ajmal House, Hayes Road, Southall, London
Made and printed by Cox and Wyman, Berks

This book is sold subject to the condition that it shall not, by way of
trade or otherwise be lent, resold, hired out, or otherwise circulated
without the publisher's prior consent in any form of binding or cover
other than that in which it is published and without a similar
condition, including this condition, being imposed upon the
subsequent purchaser.

ACKNOWLEDGEMENTS

The Compiler and Publishers of this collection would like to thank the following for granting permission to reproduce copyright material:

OODNADATTA by Ronald Oliver Brierley, copyright © R O Brierley and reproduced by kind permission of R O Brierley from *Stuff and Nonsense*, published by William Collins Pty. Ltd., Australia, 1974; PIG AND PEPPER and TWINKLE TWINKLE LITTLE BAT both by Lewis Carroll and reproduced from *Songs from Alice*, published by A & C Black Ltd., 1978; TWO SAD by William Cole, copyright © William Cole and reproduced from *A Boy Named Mary-Jane* published by Franklin Watts Ltd.; MISSING PERSON POEM, NIGHTENING and ROSEMARY'S TEETH all by Michael Dugan, copyright © M Dugan and reproduced by kind permission of Longman Cheshire Pty. Ltd., Australia from *My Old Dad*, published by Longman Cheshire, 1976; NONSENSE NUMBERS by Michael Dugan, copyright M Dugan and reproduced by kind permission of Thomas Nelson Australia from *Nonsense Numbers*, published by Ashton Scholastic Pty. Ltd., 1980; NURSERY RHYMES II by George Edward Farrow reproduced by kind permission of Century Hutchinson Ltd. from *The Missing Prince*, published by Hutchinson, 1896; ALFRED THE GREAT by Eleanor and Herbert Farjeon, copyright © E and H Farjeon and reproduced by kind permission of David Higham Associates from *The Hamish Hamilton Book of Kings*, 1964; GREAT FROG RACE by Ian Hamilton Finlay, copyright © I H Finlay and reproduced from *Second Scottish Poetry Book*, published by Oxford University Press, 1985; AWKWARD CHILD by Rose Fyleman, copyright © R Fyleman and reproduced by kind permission of The Society of Authors as the literary representative of the Estate of R Fyleman from *Fifty-One New Nursery Rhymes*, published by Basil Blackwell, 1931; THE VICAR by Carole Gardner, copyright © C Gardner and reproduced from *Children as Poets*, published by William Heinemann Limited, 1972; NOTHING by Barbara Giles, copyright © B Giles and reproduced by kind permission of B Giles from *Stuff and Nonsense*, published by William Collins Pty. Ltd., Australia, 1974; THE SEA BATTLE by Gunter Grass, copyright © Gunter Grass and reproduced from *Selected poems*, published by Secker and Warburg Ltd., 1978; ANCIENT HISTORY by Arthur

Guiterman, copyright © A Guiterman and reproduced by kind permission of L H Sclove from *Reflections on a Gift of Watermelon Pickle*, published by Scholastic Inc, USA, 1966; FOOD by Peter Hazell, copyright © P Hazell and reproduced from *Children as Poets*, published by William Heinemann Limited, 1972; BEES by Russell Hoban, copyright © R Hoban and reproduced by kind permission of David Higham Associates Ltd., from *Egg Thoughts and Other Frances Songs*, published by Faber and Faber Ltd., 1979; TED by Wilbur G Howcroft, copyright © W G Howcroft and reproduced by kind permission of W G Howcroft from *Stuff and Nonsense*, published by William Collins Pty. Ltd., Australia, 1974; WHERE HAVE YOU BEEN? by Barbara Ireson, copyright © Barbara Ireson and reproduced by kind permission of Century Hutchinson Ltd., from *Over and Over Again*, published by Beaver Books, 1984; A FUNNY MAN by Natalie Joan, copyright © Natalie Joan and reproduced from *The Faber Book of Nursery Verse*, published by Faber and Faber Ltd., 1958; "COME SIT DOWN BESIDE ME" by Michael Leunig, copyright © M Leunig and reproduced from *Stuff and Nonsense*, published by William Collins Pty. Ltd., 1974; SINK SONG by J A Lindon, copyright © J A Lindon and reproduced by kind permission of F R Lindon from *Book of Comic and Curious Verse*, published by Penguin Books Ltd.; Extract from THE MAGIC PUDDING by Norman Lindsay, copyright © Janet Glad, 1918 and reproduced by kind permission of Angus and Robertson Publishers from *The Magic Pudding*, published by Angus and Robertson Publishers, 1918; I LEFT MY HEAD and WHALE FOOD both by Lilian Moore, copyright © L Moore and reproduced by kind permission of Marian Reiner from *See My Lovely Poison Ivy*, published by Atheneum Publishers, USA, 1975; THE CAMEL and THE GUPPY by Ogden Nash, copyright © O Nash, reproduced by kind permission of André Deutsch Ltd., UK and Little Brown and Company Publishers, USA from *I Wouldn't Have Missed It* and *Verses From 1929 On* respectively and published by André Deutsch Ltd., UK and Little Brown and Co. Pub., USA, 1933 respectively; THE SQUAD CAR and THE LAST PART OF THE SQUAD CAR STORY both by Mary Neville, copyright © Mary Neville Woodrich, 1966 and reproduced by kind permission of M Neville and Random House Inc, USA from *Woody and Me*, published by Pantheon Books, USA, 1966; I NEVER HAD A PIECE OF TOAST by James Payn, copyright © J Payn and reproduced from *Junior Voices 2*, published by Penguin Books Ltd., 1970; THE PRACTICAL

JOKE, ROLLING HARVEY DOWN THE HILL, and THE
SOGGY FROG by Jack Prelutsky, copyright © J Prelutsky and
reproduced by kind permission of William Morrow and Company
Inc., USA from *Rolling Harvey Down the Hill* and *The Sheriff of
Rottenshot*, published by Greenwillow Books, USA; TIM'S
TEETH, THE SHY SHELLFISH, P. . . . and A CHILD'S
CHOICE all by Beverley Randell, copyright © Price Milburn and
reproduced from *P M Phonics*, published by Methuen Children's
Books, NZ, 1970; ENIGMA SARTORIAL by Lucy W Rhu,
copyright © L W Rhu and reproduced from *The Faber Book of
Nursery Verse*, published by Faber and Faber Ltd., 1958;
HERBERT BREEZE by Stephen Scheding, copyright © S
Scheding, and reproduced from *Stuff and Nonsense*, published
by William Collins Pty. Ltd., Australia, 1974; THE FLY IS IN by
Shel Silverstein, copyright © Snake Eye Music Ltd., 1981 and
reproduced by kind permission of Jonathan Cape Ltd., UK and
Harper and Row Publishers Inc., USA from *A Light in the Attic*,
published by Jonathan Cape Ltd., UK, and Harper and Row,
USA, 1981; SPELLING GAME by Iain Crichton Smith, copyright
© I C Smith and reproduced by kind permission of I C Smith
from *A Scottish Poetry*, published by Oxford University Press,
1983; GIGL by Arnold Spilka, copyright © A Spilka and
reproduced by kind permission of A Spilka from *A Lion I Can
Do Without*, published by Henry Zed Walck, USA, 1964;
STRETCHED OUT by Ishikawa Takuboku, copyright © I
Takuboku and reproduced by kind permission of Carl Sesar
from *Poems to Eat*, published by Kodansha International Ltd.;
JOHNNY CRACK AND FLOSSY SNAIL by Dylan Thomas,
copyright © Dylan Thomas and reproduced by kind permission
of David Higham Associates Ltd., from *Under Milk Wood*,
published by J M Dent; HARBOUR by R S Thomas, copyright
© R S Thomas and reproduced by kind permission of Grafton
Books from *Young and Old*, published by Grafton Books; BIG
JIM and COUSIN JANE both by Colin West, copyright © C
West and reproduced by kind permission of Century Hutchinson
Ltd., from *Not To Be Taken Seriously*, published by Century
Hutchinson Ltd.

**The Compiler and publishers have taken every possible
precaution to trace the owners of copyright material
reproduced in this collection. If despite this we have
inadvertently failed to identify any borrowed poem, we
would be grateful if this could be brought to our attention
for correction at the first opportunity.**

One Elephant

One elephant went out to play
Upon a spider's web one day.
He found it such enormous fun
That he called for another elephant to come.

Two elephants went out to play
Upon a lily leaf one day
They found it such enormous fun
That they called for another elephant to come.

Three elephants went out to play
Upon a roller skate one day
They fell off.

First verse anonymous
Verses two and three B Mathias

Where Have You Been?

Where have you been?
I've been to the zoo,
I saw a monkey and thought it was you.

Where have you been?
I've been there too,
And I saw a baboon who looked just like you.

Barbara Ireson

Johnny Crack and Flossie Snail

Johnnie Crack and Flossie Snail
Kept their baby in a milking pail
Flossie Snail and Johnnie Crack
One would pull it out
and one would put it back.

O it's my turn now said Flossie Snail
To take the baby from the milking pail
And it's my turn now said Johnnie Crack
To smack it on the head and put it back.

Johnnie Crack and Flossie Snail
Kept their baby in a milking pail
One would put it back
and one would pull it out
And all it had to drink was ale and stout
For Johnnie Crack and Flossie Snail
Always used to say that stout and ale
Was *good* for a baby in a milking pail.

Dylan Thomas

Stretched Out

stretched out
on the grass
minding my business —
this bird, splat!
right on my head

Ishikawa Takuboku
trans. Carl Sesar

OIC

I'm in a 10der mood today
    & feel poetic, 2;
4 fun I'll just — off a line
    & send it off 2 U.

I'm sorry you've been 6 o long;
    Don't B disconsol8;
But bear your ills with 42de,
    & they won't seem so gr8.

Anonymous

The Concert

Ladies and gentlemen 'ere we go
Kind thoughts on everyone we bestow
On us the curtain will soon descend
And so we unite
To bid you goodnight
As we're nearing the end.
As we've all done our best
We appeal to you
And we make a request,
Something you can do.
Cheers of favour we crave
Grateful we will remain,
So come with a friend
An evening to spend
And see us again.

Gertie and Flo bring your best beau,
We'll have the lights turned down very low.
Kiss if you wish, we'll understand
No one will frown if he's holding your hand.

Come in couples, come in dozens,
Bring your aunts, your nephews,
Your nieces, your cousins,
Your in-laws and your out-laws,
You can bring your neighbours
And make them pay.

So come every evening and sit on the floor
And give the glad eye to a few of us,
It's better than leaning your backs
Against walls,
And craning your neck for a view of us.
And if you've got presents to throw
On the stage
We'll bring on a decent sized sack
And we'll smile at you sweetly —
No — don't say a word
Or we'll take all your chair money back.

Time is on the wing I cannot sing with voice
unsteady,
For goodness sake an effort make, for
supper's ready.

Anonymous

I Never Had a Piece of Toast

I never had a piece of toast
Particularly long and wide,
But fell upon the sanded floor
And always on the buttered side.

James Payn

Ladles and Jellyspoons

Ladles and jellyspoons:
I come before you
To stand behind you
And tell you something
I know nothing about.

Next Friday
the day before Thursday
There'll be a ladies' meeting
For men only.

Wear your best clothes
If you haven't any,
And if you can come
Please stay home.

Admission is free,
You can pay at the door.
We'll give you a seat
You can sit on the floor.

It makes no difference
Where you sit;
The kid in the gallery
Is sure to spit.

Traditional

FREE ADMISSION

9

Twinkle Twinkle Little Bat

Twinkle, twinkle little bat!
How I wonder what you're at!
Up above the world you fly,
Like a tea-tray in the sky.
Twinkle, twinkle, twinkle, twinkle,
Twinkle, twinkle, twinkle.

Lewis Carroll

Nonsense Numbers

I thought I'd go running because it's such fun
But it gets rather lonely when there's just one
I asked a wild wombat who was mending a shoe
    If he would come with me
    And then there were two.

A barmy old bandicoot who loved making tea
    Took up his teapot
    And then there were three.

A fat wallaroo looked out of his door
    Put on his sandshoes
    And then there were four.

A gifted goanna was next to arrive
    (Doing tricks at full gallop)
    And then there were five.

A spiny anteater with his snout in a fix,
    Was rescued by wombat
    And then there were six.

Old parson platypus with feet size eleven
Hitched up his cassock
And then there were seven.

A tall emu resting his head on a gate
His legs started running
And then there were eight.

An elegant numbat sat sipping white wine,
Drained the last mouthful
And then there were nine.

A koala sat eating baked beans in his den,
Ate the last spoonful
And then there were ten.

Ten of us running in a long straggling line
"Playtime" said Wombat
And then there were nine.

Nine of us running when someone cried, "Wait!
That thing took my teapot,"
And then there were eight.

Eight of us running on feet hard and leathern,
When old parson platypus said
"Let there be seven".

Seven of us running
through tussocks and sticks
"Which way?" said goanna
And then there were six

Six of us running, Wallaroo took a dive
(Too fat to jump higher)
And then there were five.

Five of us running across a dance floor,
"See me spin!" said the numbat
And then there were four.

Four of us running down by the sea,
Koala went fishing
And then there were three.

Three of us running on feet black and blue,
A bunyip woke emu
And then there were two.

Two of us running, anteater was done —
He slept in a flower pot,
And then there was one.

One of me running.
It's really been fun,
But it gets rather lonely
When there's just one
So I stopped
And then there were none.

Michael Dugan

Pardon me

I'm a bold-legged chicken,
I'm a knock-kneed sparrow,
If I miss my bus
I'll have to go by barrow.
Stopped at the restaurant
To have a cup of tea,
Ate too many sandwiches
Ooops . . . pardon me.

Anonymous

14

The Squad Car

Woody had a birthday party,
Without any girls.
He got seven gifts
From seven boys,
And a Dick Tracy Detective Squad Car
From me.

He loved the gifts.
But most all all
He loved the squad car,
With mean-looking detectives
Painted on,
Looking out the windows
For robbers,
And a siren,
A flashing spotlight,
And a wind-up key.

The seven boys and
Woody and me
Wound and wound and wound that key.
We pulled down all the shades.
That squad car
Went circling around
Flashing its spotlight,
Screaming its siren,
Like a real car
Going to a real robbery
About ninety miles an hour!

Then
Somehow
The key got knocked
Down
A hole in the wall,
Where Daddy was
Fixing the wiring.

Oh
How we fished
For that key!
The seven boys and
Woody and me.

But it was
Down
Inside the wall.

Mother wrote a letter
To the toy company
For a new key.

They never answered.

Mother tied a magnet
To a string
And let it down
The hole in the wall.
The magnet came up
With three safety pins
And a paper clip.

Daddy tried pliers
And things
In the keyhole,
But the squad car
Just sat.

A neighbour loaned us
An old-fashioned clock key,
But it didn't fit our squad car.

Nearly one year passed.

The seven gifts were
All broken and in pieces,
But the squad car on a shelf
Was as shiny and bright
As the day it was made.

The Last Part of the Squad Car Story

It was nearly
Woody's next birthday.
Then
Mother had an
Idea.

"Why don't we get Woody
Another squad car?
Then he'll have
Two cars,
And
A key."

It was a secret
Between Mother and
Dad and
Me.

Can you guess?

The Dick Tracy Detective Squad Car,
That year's model,
Had the key
WELDED INTO
the keyhole.

Daddy said
That toy company
Must have gotten
A hundred thousand letters
About lost keys.
No wonder
They never answered.

Woody had this
Next birthday party,
Without any girls.
He got a lot of gifts
From a lot of boys,
and the *new* squad car
From me.

He said I could have
The old squad car.
I used to push it around
A little
Sometimes.

One day
I made a new friend.
On his toy shelf in a box
Of rubber bands and old
Cracker Jack prizes,
I saw
A Dick Tracy squad car key!
"I used to have
A squad car," he said.
"But it got wrecked."

I traded him three marbles
For
The key!

Mother and Dad and
Woody and
Me
Wound and wound and wound
That key!

Boy.
Do TWO squad cars
Make a lot of noise.

Mary Neville

19

Male Driver

For he's a jolly good driver,
For he's a jolly good driver,
For he's a jolly good driver,
He never misses a bump!

Anonymous

Come Sit Down Beside Me

"Come sit down beside me"
I said to myself,
And although it doesn't make sense,
I held my own hand
As a small sign of trust
And together we sat on the fence.

Michael Leunig

Sink Song

Scouring out the porridge pot,
Round and round and round!

Out with all the scraith and scoopery,
Lift the eely ooly droopery,
Chase the glubbery slubbery gloopery
Round and round and round!

Out with all the doleful dithery,
Ladle out the slimy slithery,
Hunt and catch the hithery slithery,
Round and round and round!

Out with all the obbly gubbly,
On the stove it burns so bubbly,
Use the spoon and use it doubly,
Round and round and round!

J A Lindon

Pig and Pepper

"Speak roughly to your little boy,
And beat him when he sneezes:
He only does it to annoy
Because he knows it teases."
Wow! wow! wow!

"I speak severely to my boy,
I beat him when he sneezes;
For he can thoroughly enjoy
The pepper when he pleases!"
Wow! wow! wow!

Lewis Carroll

Riddle

Two legs sat upon three legs,
With one leg in his lap;
In comes four legs,
And runs away with one leg.
Up jumps two legs,
Catches up three legs,
Throws it after four legs,
And makes him bring one leg back.

Anonymous

one leg = leg of lamb
two legs = a man
three legs = a stool
four legs = a dog

The Guppy

Whales have calves,
Cats have kittens,
Bears have cubs,
Bats have bittens.
Swans have cygnets,
Seals have puppies,
But guppies just have little guppies.

Ogden Nash

The Shy Shellfish

The shellfish lives
in a shiny shell.
He shuts his door.
He shuts it well.
The shellfish is shy
because he's delicious
and the ocean is full
of hungry fishes.

Beverley Randell

Cousin Jane

Yesterday my cousin Jane
Said she was an aeroplane,
But I wanted further proof —
So I pushed her off the roof.

Colin West

I Left My Head

I left my head
somewhere
today.
Put it down for
just
a minute.
Under the
table?
On a chair?
Wish I were
able
to say
where.
Everything I need
is
in it!

Lilian Moore

Thunder and Lightning

The thunder crashed
The lightning flashed
And all the world was shaken;
The little pig
Curled up his tail
And ran to save his bacon.

Anonymous

The Frog

What a wonderful bird the frog are –
When he sit, he stand almost;
When he hop, he fly almost.
He ain't got no sense hardly;
He ain't got no tail hardly either.
When he sit, he sit on what he ain't got —
almost.

Anonymous

I Wish

Oh I wish I was a little drop of mud,
Oh I wish I was a little drop of mud,
I'd oozy and I'd squoozy under everybody's shoes-y
Oh I wish I was a little drop of mud.

Oh I wish I was a little cake of soap
Oh I wish I was a little cake of soap
I'd slippy and I'd slide-y under everybody's hide-y
Oh I wish I was a little cake of soap.

Oh I wish I was a little mosquito,
Oh I wish I was a little mosquito,
I'd hide-y and I'd bite-y under everybody's nightie
Oh I wish I was a little mosquito.

Oh I wish I was a little English sparrow,
Oh I wish I was a little English sparrow,
I'd sit up on the spire and I'd spit on all the choir
Oh I wish I was a little English sparrow.

Oh I wish I was a fish-y in the sea,
Oh I wish I was a fish-y in the sea,
I'd swim around so cute without a bathing suit,
Oh I wish I was a fish-y in the sea.

Anonymous

Longing

I wish I was a little grub
With whiskers round my tummy
I'd climb into a honey-pot
And make my tummy gummy.

Anonymous

David and Goliath

Goliath of Gath
With helmet of brath
Wath theated one day
Upon the green grath.

When up thkipped thlim David
A thervant of Thaul,
And thaid I will thmite thee
Although I am thmall.

Thlim David thkipped down
To the edge of the thtream,
And from it'th thmooth thurface
Five thmooth thtones he took,

He loothened hith corthetth
And thevered hith head,
And all Ithrael thouted —
"Yippee" Goliath ith dead!

Anonymous

The Vicar

The Vicar is coming just after tea
But he is not coming just to see me,
I think he is coming to watch the TV,
For we like the Lone Ranger and so does he.

Carole Gardner (10)

Oodnadatta

Oodnadatta
Parramatta
Names to make your tonsils chatter —
Tonsils chatter,
Silly patter
Oodnadatta
Parramatta.

Ronald Oliver Brierley

The Fly is in

The fly is in
The milk is in
The bottle is in
The fridge is in
The kitchen is in
The house is in
The town.

The worm is under
The ground is under
The grass is under
The blanket is under
The diaper* is under
The baby is under
The tree.

The flea is on
The dog is on
The quilt is on
The bed is on
The carpet is on
The floor is on
The ground.

The bee is bothering
The puppy is bothering
The dog is bothering
The cat is bothering
The baby is bothering
Mama is bothering
Me.

Shel Silverstein

* A diaper is a baby's nappy.

One Fine Day

One fine day in the middle of the night.
Two dead men got up to fight.
One blind man to see fair play
Two dumb men to shout "Hooray".
A three-legged donkey, passing by,
Kicked the blind man in the eye.
Sent him through a brick wall
Into an empty bucket of cold water where he
scalded himself.

Anonymous

Riddles

The land was white
The seed was black;
It'll take a good scholar
To riddle me that.

(print on a page)

As I went over London Bridge
Upon a cloudy day
I met a fellow clothed in yellow.
I took him up and sucked his blood,
And threw his skin away.

(blood orange)

On yonder hill there is a red deer,
The more you shoot it, the more you may,
You cannot drive that deer away.

(the rising sun)

Traditional

A Child's Choice

It's "Cheese Please"
for Dad and Mum . . .
Now I'd choose chocolate
or chewing gum.
Or I'd choose chicken.
I'd choose these.
Or chops. Or chips.
But THEY choose cheese.

Beverley Randell

Three Ghostesses

There were three ghostesses
Sitting on postesses
Eating buttered toastesses
And greasing their fistesses
Right up to their wristesses
Weren't they beastesses
To make such feastesses.

Anonymous

The Soggy Frog

The toad's abode
is by the road,
the frog's abode
is boggy —

explaining why
the toad seems dry,
and why the frog
seems soggy.

Jack Prelutsky

Old Hank

For a lark,
For a prank,
Old Hank
Walked the plank.
These bubbles mark
O
O
O
O
O
Where Hank sank.

Anonymous

Two Sad

It's such a shock, I almost screech,
When I find a worm inside my peach!
But then, what *really* makes me blue
Is to find a worm who's bit in two!

William Cole

The Lobster

'Tis the voice of the Lobster: I heard him declare,
"You have baked me too brown, I must sugar my hair."
As a duck with its eyelids, so he with his nose
Trims his belt and his buttons, and turns out his toes.

I passed by his garden, and marked, with
one eye,
How the Owl and the Oyster were sharing
a pie;
While the Duck and the Dodo, the Lizard
and Cat,
Were swimming in milk round the brim of
a hat.

Lewis Carroll

Bees

Honey bees are very tricky —
Honey doesn't make them sticky.

Russell Hoban

A Funny Man

One day a funny kind of man
Came walking down the street.
He wore a shoe upon his head,
And hats upon his feet.

He raised the shoe and smiled at me,
His manners were polite;
But never had I seen before
Such a funny-sounding sight.

He said, "Allow me to present
Your Highness with a rose."
And taking out a currant bun
He held it to my nose.

I staggered back against the wall,
And then I answered, "Well!
I never saw a rose with such
A funny-looking smell."

He then began to sing a song,
And sat down on the ground;
You never heard in all your life
Such a funny-feeling sound.

"My friend, why do you wear two hats
Upon your feet?" I said.
He turned the other way about,
And hopped home on his head.

Natalie Joan

GREAT FROG RACE

A F L O P

Ian Hamilton Finlay

Spelling Game

If the plural of house is houses
and the plural of mouse is mice
why then the plural of grouses
should surely be written as grice.

and if the plural of deer is deer
and the plural of fish is fish
then the plural of beer should be beer
and the plural of dish should be dish.

If mouses run over our houses
and eat up our loaves and our scones
why then our lice should be louses
and our phones should be sounded as phons.

Iain Crichton Smith

PRS

(Add one vowel to the following letters and you have a carving found in a church in Wales)

P R S V R Y P R F C T M N
V R K P T H S P R C P T S T N

Anonymous

Answer: Persevere ye perfect men
ever keep these precepts ten

Puddin' Song

"O, who would be a puddin',
  A puddin' in a pot,
A puddin' which is stood on
  A fire which is hot?
  O, sad indeed the lot
  Of puddin's in a pot.

"I wouldn't be a puddin'
  If I could be a bird,
If I could be a wooden
  Doll, I wouldn't say a word.
  Yes, I have often heard
  It's grand to be a bird.

"But as I am a puddin',
  A puddin' in a pot,
I hope you get the stomachache
  For eatin' me a lot,
  I hope you get it hot,
  You puddin'-eatin' lot!"

Norman Lindsay

51

Weekend

Friday night is my delight
And so is Saturday morning.
But Sunday night — it gives me a fright:
There's school on Monday morning.

Anonymous

The Minister in the Pulpit

The minister in the pulpit,
He couldn't say his prayers,
He laughed and he giggled,
And he fell down the stairs.
The stairs gave a crack,
And he broke his humpy back,
And all the congregation
Went "Quack, quack, quack".

Traditional

Gigl

A pigl
wigl
if
u
tigl

Arnold Spilka

Nursery Rhymes II

Hey diddle diddle the cat couldn't fiddle,
The cow turned her back on the moon,
The little dog said: "This is very poor sport",
And the dish had a row with the spoon.

Simple Simon went a-skating
On a pond in June.
"Dear me," he cried, "this water's wet,
I fear I've come too soon."

Simple Simon saw a sparrow
Flying through the air.
"Why shouldn't I have wings?" he cried;
"I'm sure it isn't fair."

So Simple Simon bought some feathers,
Made a pair of wings;
And now he's broken both his legs
He calls them "foolish things".

Simple Simon bought a gun,
"To shoot some game," he said.
He held the gun the wrong way round,
And shot himself instead.

George Edward Farrow

Ancient History

I hope the old Romans
Had painful abdomens.

I hope that the Greeks
Had toothache for weeks.

I hope the Egyptians
Had chronic conniptions.

I hope that the Arabs
Were bitten by scarabs.

I hope that the Vandals
Had thorns in their sandals.

I hope that the Persians
Had gout in all versions.

I hope that the Medes
Were kicked by their steeds.

They started the fuss
And left it to us!

Arthur Guiterman

Tombstone

At rest beneath this slab of stone,
  Lies stingy Jimmy Wyett
He died one morning just at ten
  And saved a dinner by it.

                On a grave in Falkirk

At the Zoo

First I saw the white bear,
then I saw the black;
Then I saw the camel
with a hump upon his back;
Then I saw the grey wolf,
with mutton in his maw;
Then I saw the wombat waddle in the straw;
Then I saw the elephant a-waving of his trunk;
Then I saw the monkeys
— mercy how unpleasantly they — smelt!

William Makepeace Thackeray

Rolling Harvey Down the Hill

Harvey whimpers, Harvey whines
and Harvey is a pest,
Harvey tells us every day
that Harvey is the best.
Harvey's always butting in,
his mouth is never still,
so Tony, Lumpy, Will and me
rolled Harvey down the hill.

See him rolling, rolling, rolling,
see him rolling down the hill.
All the way from top to bottom.
we rolled Harvey down the hill.

Jack Prelutsky

Abey! See de Gol'fish?

A.B.C.D.	Gol'fish?
M.N.O.	Gol'fish.
S.D.R.	Gol'fish.
R.D.R.	Gol'fish!

Anonymous

Food

I hav for breakfast Weetabix
I hav for lunch some meat
I have for tea 2 sosajis
And thats enuf to eat.

Peter Hazell (5)

Through the Teeth

Through the teeth,
Past the gums,
Look out, stomach,
Here it comes!

Anonymous

Sticky Veg

I eat my peas with honey
I've done it all my life
It makes the peas taste funny
But it keeps them on the knife.

Anonymous

The Practical Joke

Harvey likes to practice knots
with different kinds of string.
He bragged to me and Willie
he could tie up anything.

"Let me try my knots on you,"
he asked us both one day.
Willie wanted to show him up
and so we said OK.

Harvey took some clothesline
and he tied us both to trees,
he wound it round our shoulders
and made knots behind our knees.

He tied us very carefully
with lots and lots of rope.
"Can you get loose?" he asked us,
And Willie answered, "Nope!"

"You're positive you can't get free?"
I said, "We're tied too tight."
Then Harvey grinned and smugly said,
"I guess I did it right."

Harvey pinched and tickled us,
we yelled, "That isn't fair!"
He laughed and pulled our trousers down
and left us standing there.

Jack Prelutsky

Watch it!

Small is the wren
Black is the rook,
Great is the sinner,
That steals this book.

Traditional

Accident

Ooey Gooey was a worm,
A little worm was he —
He sat upon the railway track
The train he didn't see.
Ooey-gooey.

Anonymous

Obituary

A doggie stole a sausage
When he was underfed.
The butcher saw him take it
And now poor doggie's dead.

And all the little doggies
They gathered there that night
They built a little tombstone
And on it they did write . . .

A doggie stole a sausage
When he was underfed,
The butcher saw him take it
And now poor doggie's dead.

And all the little doggies . . . .

Anonymous

A Pin

A pin has a head, but has no hair;
A clock has a face, but no mouth there;
Needles have eyes, but they cannot see;
A fly* has a trunk without lock or key;
A timepiece may lose, but cannot win;
A cornfield dimples without a chin;
A hill has no leg, but has a foot;
A wine-glass a stem, but not a root;
Rivers run, though they have no feet;
A saw has teeth, but it does not eat;
Ash-trees have keys, yet never a lock;
And baby crows, without being a cock.

Christina Rosetti

* a fly is a form of horse-drawn vehicle

Peanuts

A peanut sat on the railroad track,
 His head was all a-flutter;
Along came a train — the 9.15 —
 Toot, toot, peanut butter!

Anonymous

P...

Pippa and Penelope
Saw a poodle pup.
Pippa stooped to pat him.
Penny picked him up.

Beverley Rande

Awkward Child

She fell into the bath-tub,
She fell into the sink
She fell into the raspberry jam
And came-out-pink.

They took her down to Kensington
And left her in the rain;
She fell into the Serpentine
And was not seen again.

Rose Fyleman

Music

There's music in a hammer
There's music in a nail,
There's music in a pussycat
When you step on her tail!

Anonymous

Missing Person Poem

Would anyone knowing the
whereabouts of Algernon
Wilberforce Smith, last
seen in the Treasury
Gardens Fountain wearing
scarlet satin pyjamas
please phone 99 9999. He
is fourteen metres
tall and weighs seventeen
tonnes. No distinguishing
features.

Michael Dugan

I'm Goin' Down to the Railroad

I'm goin' down to the railroad
Lay my head on the track
But if I see the train a-comin'
I'll jerk it back.

Anonymous

Herbert Breeze

Herbert Breeze
Had three exploding knees
One he kept as a spare
The other two he wore everywhere.

Stephen Scheding

Counting Out Rhymes

Eeny, pheeny, figgery, fegg,
Deely, dyly, ham and egg.
Calico back and stony rock,
Arlum, barlum, bock!

As I was walking down the lake,
I met a little rattlesnake,
I gave him so much jelly-cake
It made his little belly ache.
One, two, three, out goes she!

Traditional

The Camel

The camel has a single hump;
  The dromedary, two;
Or else the other way around,
  I'm never sure. Are you?

Ogden Nash

Big Jim

When we play cricket, we don't let Jim bowl;
And when we play baseball, we don't let Jim
bat.
But when we play football, we put Jim in goal,
For balls can't get past him, because Jim's so
fat.

Colin West

Duel

One fine day in the middle of the night
Two dead men got up to fight
Back to back they faced each other
Drew their swords and shot each other.

Anonymous

Harbour

a harbour with the
boats going in and out
at top speed their sirens
blowing and their funnels trailing
long smoke and the tousled
bluejackets of the waves emptying
their pockets to the wind's
hornpipe and far down
in the murky basements the turning
of bright bodies smooth
as a bell mermaids you
say but I say
fish

R S Thomas

Entertainment

I went to the pictures tomorrow
And took a front seat at the back.
I fell from the floor to the ceiling
And hurt the front part of my back.

I went round a corner sideways
And saw a dead donkey die,
I took out my revolver to stab him
And he caught me a kick in the eye.

Anonymous

Nothing

If nobody had no body.
Nobody would know
No one could see anyone
Nowhere could they go —
No one would walk up to no one
To look him in the eye,
If nobody heard no voices
No one would reply.

Barbara Giles

Spring

Spring is here
The grass is riz
I wonder where the birdies is.
The birdies they is on the wing
But that's absurd —
I always thought the wing was on the bird!

Anonymous

Rosemary's Teeth

Rosemary Freeth
had holes in her teeth,
deeper than ten metre rules.
So she said with a shout —
"Take all my teeth out
and I'll sell them for swimming pools."

Michael Dugan

There was an old man . . .

There was an old man,
And he had a calf,
And that's half.

He took him from the stall,
And put him on the wall,
And that's all.

Anonymous

The Sea Battle

An American aircraft carrier
and a Gothic cathedral
simultaneously sank each other
in the middle of the Pacific.
To the last
the young curate played on the organ.
Now aeroplanes and angels hang in the air
and have nowhere to land.

Gunter Grass
trans. Michael Hamburger

My Father

My father owns the butcher shop,
My mother cuts the meat,
And I'm the little hot dog
That runs around the street.

Anonymous

Alfred the Great

Chill, shrill,
wind bloweth,
up hill
Alfred goeth,
by Dane
down-trodden,
heart, brain,
skin sodden.

Rain raineth,
sludge sludgeth,
pain paineth,
Alfred trudgeth.

At hut
King knocketh,
old slut
unlocketh.
"Help, kind
crone, prithee!"
"Pack, hind!
Off with 'ee!"

Slut grumbleth,
Alfred prayeth,
slut mumbleth,
Alfred stayeth.

By glow,
King stretcheth,
rye dough
slut fetcheth,
no whit
King heedeth
whiles it
slut kneadeth.

Heart warmeth,
Alfred lieth,
storm stormeth,
Alfred drieth.

"Watch bake
dough, fellow,
till cake
turn'th yellow,
while I
brave cruel
cold sky
fetching fuel."

Glow gloweth,
gleam gleameth,
slut goeth,
Alfred dreameth.

In fire,
future seeth:
King's ire
Dane fleeth,
King's arm
Dane feeleth,
flame's charm
heart healeth.

Alfred thinketh,
hope returneth,
fire winketh,
cake burneth.

* * *

"Lout! block!
lackwit! looby!
stick! stock!
bull-head! booby!"

"Come, thing,"
Alfred sayeth,
"thy King
pardon prayeth!"

Slut moaneth,
Weepeth, squealeth,
whineth, groaneth,
waileth, kneeleth.

Thwack! thwack!
slut clouteth!
"Cake's black!"
slut shouteth.
"Fool! dolt!"
King quaileth!
"Clod! colt!"
slut raileth.

Slut growleth,
rateth, ranteth,
screameth, scowleth,
prateth, panteth.

"Up, slut!
wherefore grovel?
Sweet hut!
bless thy hovel!"

Birds trill,
cock croweth,
down hill
Alfred goeth.

Sky cleareth,
leaf drippeth
sun cheereth,
Alfred skippeth.

*Herbert and
Eleanor Farjeon*

Enigma Sartorial

Consider the Penguin.
He's smart as can be —
Dressed in his dinner clothes
Permanently.
You never can tell,
When you see him about,
If he's just coming in
Or just going out!

Lucy W Rhu

Silence

A very wise bird with a very long beak
Sat solemnly blinking away.
When asked why it was that he never would
speak,
he replied: "I have nothing to say".

Anonymous

Old Hogan's Goat

Old Hogan's goat
Was feeling fine,
He ate a red shirt
Right off the line.

I took a stick
And beat his back,
And tied him to
A railway track.

A speeding train
Was drawing nigh,
Old Hogan's goat
Was doomed to die.

He gave an aw-
ful shriek of pain,
Coughed up that shirt
And flagged that train.

Traditional

Mother, Mother

Mother, may I go and bathe?
Yes, my darling daughter.
Hang your clothes on yonder tree,
But don't go near the water.

Mother, may I go to swim?
Yes, my darling daughter.
Fold your clothes up neat and trim,
But don't go near the water.

Anonymous

Tim's Teeth

Tim had twenty
Teeth on Tuesday. . .
Ate a toffee. . .
Got a fright. . . .
Tim had twenty
Teeth on Tuesday. . . .
Tim had nineteen,
Tuesday night.

Beverley Randell

Nightening

When you wake up at night
and it's dark and frightening,
    don't be afraid —
    turn on the lightening.

Michael Dugan

Where?

On a mule you find two feet behind
Two feet you find before;
You stand behind before you find
What the two behind be for.

Anonymous

Amen

Ashes to ashes
Dust to dust
Oil those brains
Before they rust.

Anonymous

Ted

A bandy-legged man named Ted
Put hay and chaff beside his bed.
A thoughtful and a kindly deed,
To see his nightmares got a feed.

Wilbur G Howcroft

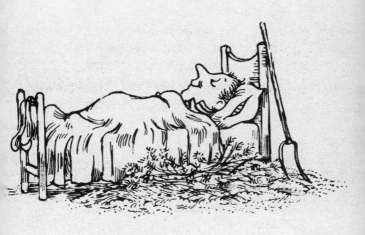

Whale Food

A whale liked to eat portions double.
Nothing he ate gave him trouble.
But he just couldn't cope
With *two* bars of soap.
And he now blows a whale of a bubble.

Lilian Moore

Moo

Oh what would you do if you had a cow
Who never said "Moo!"
but preferred "Bow-wow";
Who played the guitar and lived in a sty,
And put on galoshes to keep her feet dry?

Anonymous

Carol For Christmas

While shepherds washed their socks by night
All seated on the ground.
A bar of Sunlight soap came down
And soapsuds rose all round.

While shepherds washed their socks by night
While watching ITV,
An angel of the Lord came down
And switched to BBC.

Anonymous

100

My Dog

I've got a dog as thin as a rail,
He's got fleas all over his tail;
Every time his tail goes flop,
The fleas on the bottom all hop to the top.

Anonymous

Index of Titles and First Lines

103

Index of Poets